Master Wonhyo

An Overview of His Life and Teachings

Published by Diamond Sutra Recitation Group

Publisher Kim, Jae-Woong

Author Jeong, Byeong-Jo

Printed and Bound by Samjung Munhwasa

Chungjeong-ro 37-18, Seodaemun-gu, Seoul

First print, December 2010

ISBN: 978-0-9797263-7-8

Note on Romanization

The Romanization of Korean words in this book follows the McCune-Reischauer system, except in the case of prominent figures and place names for which alternative usages are better known.

When you have read this booklet, please donate it to a library or school so that it can be shared with others. Thank you.

Contents

Timeline of Korean History

BC 700000~BC 80000	Paleolithic Period
BC 8000~BC 2000	Neolithic Period
BC 2333~BC 108	Old Choson Dynasty: The First Kingdom of Korea (Bronze Age & Iron Age)
BC 57~AD 668	Three Kingdoms Period: Koguryo, Paekche and Silla
668	Three Kingdoms unified under Silla
668~ 935	Unified Silla
918~1392	Koryo Dynasty
1392~ 1910	Choson Dynasty
1910~1945	Japanese Occupation
1948	Korea divided into North (DPRK) and South (ROK)
1950~1953	Korean War
1986	South Korea hosts Asian Games in Seoul
1988	South Korea hosts Summer Olympic Games in Seoul
1995	South Korea joins OECD
2002	South Korea and Japan Co-host 2002 FIFA World Cup
2005	South Korea hosts APEC Summit in Pusan
2010	South Korea hosts G20 Summit in Seoul

I. Preface

As humanity moves towards unprecedented levels of material wealth and sophistication in the 21st century, personal and collective ethics have deteriorated. In the single-minded pursuit of convenience and rationalism, we find ourselves in a world where everything is commoditized and standardized. All around the globe, as inequality of wealth and diplomatic tensions escalate, enmity between religions and sects is also growing. Amid these turbulent times, we turn to the life and philosophy of Master Wonhyo.

Buddhism was transmitted to Silla (57 B.C.-935 A.D.) in the early 6th century. Silla was the last of the Three Ancient Kingdoms of Korea to be introduced to the new teaching. Initially, due to the complexity of its doctrines and the unfamiliarity of its customs, Buddhism was viewed with deep suspicion by the majority of the public. However, successive kings of Silla showed an increasing interest in the practice and study of the new religion, and supported its propagation as a means of uniting the country. As a result, Buddhism gradually took root within people's hearts. The early pioneers were Ichadon, Ado, Wongwang and Chajang. Thereafter, Wonhyo and Uisang are credited with laying the solid foundations of Buddhism in Korea.

Of these men, Master Wonhyo (617-686 A.D.) is regarded as the most important. His influence went beyond Korea, and he is held in high esteem in East Asia. In his lifetime, he analyzed ten of the most controversial issues among the Buddhist sects of the day, and resolved their differing belief systems into what he called 'One Vehicle Buddhism'. Since then, the tendency of Korean Buddhism has been towards concordance rather than fragmentation.

Wonhyo was one of history's great intellects, and accumulated a remarkable amount of knowledge within his lifetime. He lived outside the confines of authority and form, choosing to live a life of *muae* or "non-hindrance", face to face with reality. He tried to remove the distinction between sacred and secular, and associated freely with ordinary people, even taking part in music and dancing. This is one of the reasons why he continues to exert influence and commands a respect comparable to famous artists of modern times.

In the portrait of Wonhyo, enshrined at the Kouzanji Temple at Kyoto in Japan, his appearance is that of a fiery young warrior, and not, as one might expect, that of a demure scholar or idealized Buddhist monk. It is related that "his deeds and words were sometimes wildly immoral, transgressing the accepted norms". Despite his unusual appearance and behaviour, we can infer that his life was not immoral in the conventional sense, but merely that it went beyond established boundaries. For this reason, the accounts of his life always contain an element of surprise. He is like a person from an unfamiliar future age, rather than a figure from the past.

Wonhyo is believed to have written 100 works, comprising 240 volumes in total (some sources say 85 works and 181 volumes). Although the originals of these works have not survived, written copies and wood-block prints of the main works do exist, providing a valuable insight into his philosophy. Wonhyo's works represent a pinnacle in the Mahayana Buddhist tradition of East Asia. They encompass every variation of Indian Buddhism that reached China, Korea and Japan, following the establishment of Early Buddhism after the Nirvana of Shakyamuni Buddha.

After several hundred years, the fundamental schools of teaching that developed following Shakyamuni Buddha's ministry became a smaller number of schools, such as the Middle-Way, Consciousness-Only and Flower Ornament.

As these diverse strands of thought entered China through various means and over different periods of time, many different sects were formed, and disputes and rivalry became more common. Although he never studied abroad, Wonhyo eventually mastered the various Buddhist belief systems prevalent in the surrounding countries, and was able to approach them with a degree of objectivity. His own ideas eventually came to exert a profound influence in the neighbouring countries of China and Japan.

Wonhyo never belonged to a particular sect, as we can see from the way he lived his life. In his writings, we sense an endeavor to break away from the 'individual subject', a key issue in modern philosophy. A thinker who went beyond mere theory and put his teachings into practice, there is much that Wonhyo's life can teach us now.

Wonhyo faced a great deal of criticism from academics during his day. Nonetheless, he stands alone in Korean Buddhism's history of two thousand years, not only for his profound teachings and beliefs, but also his remarkable way of life, which was a living testimony to these beliefs. Though thoroughly versed in various schools of thought, he rose above the sectarian formalism that is wedded to one particular doctrine. For this reason he is known as the founder of 'Syncretic Buddhism'. The ideal he pursued was a perfect, holistic understanding of the real and ideal. Therefore he proposed 'Harmonizing-Disputations' (*Hwajeang*), and practiced 'Non-Hindrance' (*Muae*). Within the vast scope of his scholarship, the sophistication of his logic, and his deeds and way of living, which ultimately surpassed his theories, we find the merits of a great life that may be appreciated in any age, and in any civilisation.

II. Historical Background

In the 7th century, when Master Wonhyo was alive, Eurasia was entering a new era. Sui China had made a number of unsuccessful invasions of Koguryo Korea, and in the end gave way to the Tang Dynasty. The power of this new ruling family extended from Central Asia to the Far East. In the Middle East, after the founding of Islam by the prophet Muhammad under the tenet "All are equal before Allah", the Arabs drove out the Byzantine Empire to form the first Islamic Saracen Empire. Meanwhile, Silla (57 B.C.-935 A.D.) unified the Korean peninsula after an intense struggle with Paekche (18 B.C.-660 A.D.) and Koguryo (37 B.C.-668 A.D.), the other two ancient kingdoms of Korea.

The interplay between East and West increased considerably during this period as well. By land, the Silk Road ran from the Chinese continent and the Steppe Route in the north all the way to the Mediterranean. The Silk Road was established in the 1st century B.C., and it was by this route that the Gandhara arts, in which Buddha is represented in human form in a style influenced by Greek art, were introduced to Central Asia, China and Korea. By sea, the Marine Route served the southern Eurasian Continent. Persian merchant ships sailed to Southeast Asia and traded as far as the Chinese coast.

These three main routes of commerce – the Silk Road, the Steppe Road and the Marine Route – effectively made the world smaller, and the birth of a new era in world history began. While some believe this to have occurred during the Age of Sail in the 15th century, when Europeans explored the New Continents of

America and Africa and established routes for circumnavigation, this is a more European-centric notion.

Meanwhile in China, Buddhism itself was entering a new phase. Towards the middle of the 7th century, the famous Buddhist monk Xuanzang[1] returned after 17 years of study in India (629~645). Once home, he made a translation of 73 of the Buddhist scriptures, which nowadays are known as the 'New Translations'. This new canon was more extensive than the previous translations, and brought about the rise of a new academic tradition in the Buddhist sects of Tang China.

After unifying Korea, Silla had assimilated the Buddhist practices of the other two Kingdoms. Further stimulated by the new movements within Tang China, countless Buddhist masters appeared and began to propagate the Dharma. As the newly translated scriptures were introduced and studied more deeply, the foundations of a new Buddhism unique to Silla were laid. Master Wonhyo of Silla acquired a comprehensive view of the many diverse Buddhist systems and traditions of the time. Not only did he seamlessly harmonize the real and the ideal, but he also perfected the development of Korean Buddhism.

---

[1] Xuanzang is the main character in *Journey to the West*, one of the Four Great Classical Novels of Chinese literature, well known for the character of the "monkey king" Sun Wukong.

III. Wonhyo's Early Life

1. Chestnut Valley

Wonhyo was born in 617 A.D., during the reign of King Chinpyong (579-632). Exactly 90 years before, Buddhism had gained official recognition in Silla under King Pophung. Wonhyo's birthplace was Puljichon (Buddha Land Village) in the Amnyang-gun County of North Kyongsang Province. The village is also said to have been known as Palji (Awakening of Wisdom). As these names suggest, it was a region strongly associated with Buddhist practice.

Wonhyo's grandfather was called Sir Ingpi, and his father, Soldamnal was a government official. Soldamnal and his wife had been blessed with everything they could wish for except a child. Each dawn, his wife prayed devoutly to Buddha to send her a son or daughter. One night, perhaps in answer to her prayers, she had a very auspicious dream. The largest of the stars in the sky sped down from heaven like an arrow and pierced her bosom. Startled, she awoke and told her husband, who was very pleased and considered it an omen foretelling the birth of a child. Indeed, soon after the dream, she began to show signs of pregnancy.

One day, as she was passing the Chestnut Valley, she suddenly fell into labour. As it was too late to return home, Soldamnal took off his outer garments, and hung them on the branch of a chestnut tree as a makeshift screen, scattering dry grass underneath. The female attendants helped to deliver the child, and Soldamnal prayed that his wife might give birth safely.

Just then, five clouds of brilliant, contrasting hues enveloped the makeshift shelter where the lady was giving birth. The clouds soon filled the entire valley, and shortly afterwards the sound of a new-born child was heard. The name given to the child was Sodang (Wonhyo, the name he is known by today, literally means 'break of dawn').

This story has certain elements in common with the story of the birth of the Shakyamuni Buddha. According to the tale, Queen Maya fell into labour by the Lumbini Grove on the way to her parents' home in Koli, and her son the Crown Prince was born under a screened ashoka tree (a sala tree). On this occasion, it is said that an auspicious sunbeam stretched out from heaven towards the earth, and reached the new born son. Wonhyo was also born under a chestnut tree (also called the sala tree), and his birth was accompanied by a similar omen.

2. Pursuing the Spiritual Path

Sodang was a gifted child, described as a prodigy who "could infer ten things after learning one". Because he was also a talented horse-rider and javelin-thrower, he became a member of the Hwarang (lit. Flower Youth), a group of elite young soldiers who underwent rigorous training in body and mind. Once he embarked on the spiritual path, he took the name 'Wonhyo', and turned his house into a monastery, which he called Chogae. He also built a temple beside the sala chestnut tree that had given him shelter during his birth, naming it Salasa.

It is not clear why he decided to renounce the world at the age of 15, while he was still serving as a Hwarang, nor how long he deliberated before making the decision. One story is that he witnessed the death of a fellow Hwarang in war, and after realizing the briefness of human life, began to pursue the reality beyond the grave.

Wonhyo belonged to the lower Kolpum ranks of Silla society, and his prospects of promotion to a high position in government were severely restricted. Some believe that Buddhism offered members of the Kolpum the prospect of raising themselves in society, transcending the limits imposed by the hierarchical system.

However, to explain Wonhyo's pursuit of the path simply as a means of social progression is superficial. For those who are truly devoted to the spiritual path, worldly success and fame are not objects in themselves. To pursue the path, one must prize a virtuous life above all, and in this context distinctions between people made on the basis of time, place and position are meaningless.

He wrote a guide for young spiritual seekers, called *Palsim Suhaengjang* (The Awakening of Faith and Practice), and it remains a source of inspiration and faith for those who are new to Buddhism. These writings are filled with his own experiences of practice, and the mindset of his younger days.

High mountains and rough peaks are where wise men dwell. Green pines and deep mountain valleys are home to those who practice. When hungry, they pick fruit from trees to calm an empty stomach. When thirsty, they quench their thirst with water from the running stream. Though we feed this body with delicacies and nurture it with care, it is certain to fail us eventually. And though we cover it with fine clothes, the time will come when our lives must cease.

A rocky cave that resonates with echoing sounds, make this your hall of recitation. The wild geese that cry in solitude, make these the joyful companions of your mind. Though your knees are cold and numb from continuous bowing, have no thought for a fire. Though your empty stomach feels severed from the body, have no thought to look for food. Before you know it, you will be a hundred years old, so why do you neglect to learn? Could life ever be long enough for us to idle it away, and neglect our studies?

As a spiritual seeker, it is believed that Wonhyo must have been taught by eminent masters in every field of practice, and it is very probable that he studied under renowned monks such as Nangji, Podok and Hyegong. The word 'teacher' in Buddhism is usually associated with the lineage of the Dharma and its continued passage from master to disciple. In Wonhyo's case, however, it appears that he had neither a dedicated teacher nor a student, and this is highly significant. A student learns from the teacher, and becomes teacher to his own student. In the same way, a parent raises a child, who later becomes a parent, and so the cycle continues. The relationship between teacher and student, and the continued handing down of tradition by means of this relationship, is a common theme of human life, constantly repeating itself. To have no teacher, therefore, means to awaken enlightenment by oneself, and to exist outside the law of cause and effect. If one is not tied to the laws of cause and effect, 'by oneself' here means 'eternity'. To say that Wonhyo did not follow a teacher, therefore, is to say that he was a being that transcended this world and its natural laws.

IV. The Quest to Study Abroad

1. Wonhyo and Uisang

The spiritual path is not necessarily pursued alone, and spiritual seekers can benefit and learn from the company of fellow practitioners. Wonhyo had such a companion in Master Uisang (625-702). Although Wonhyo and Uisang differed in terms of family background, personality, methods of practice and points of emphasis, each held the other's character and learning in high regard.

There are many stories in which Master Wonhyo and Uisang appear together. The phrase "Thus spake Master Wonhyo..." appears repeatedly in accounts of their devoted studies of Flower Ornament Buddhism, and Uisang's disciples frequently cite Wonhyo's sayings. When Master Uisang founded the Naksansa Temple, Wonhyo is said to have visited soon afterwards to offer up prayers.

Born of a noble family in 625, Master Uisang renounced the world at the age of 19 in the Hwangboksa Temple in Kyongju, the capital of Silla. In, 661, Uisang traveled to Tang China in search of a wider education. It is said that Uisang had to cross rough seas to arrive at Dengzhou, where he stayed for a few days at the home of Liu Zhiren, a lay-follower. Liu Zhiren had a beautiful daughter named Shanmiao, who fell in love with Uisang at first sight. However, she was unable to move the spiritual seeker, whose resolve to study was unbreakable. After leaving the home of Liu Zhiren, Uisang went to Changan, capital city of the Tang, where he stayed for ten years studying the new schools of Buddhism.

For ten years, Shanmiao continued vainly in her love. Learning that Uisang intended to stop at her father's house before returning to Silla, she prepared a box of clothes, dishes and utensils as a gift for the master, and awaited his arrival. As it happened, Uisang boarded the ship before she could give him the gift. Standing on the shore, she prayed, "If my mind is sincere towards the Master, and wholly pure, may this box reach his hands". She threw the box into the waves, and it was carried safely to its destination. She continued, "May this body become a dragon to protect the ship which carries the Master, and help him in his service to the Buddha". She then leapt into the sea, and immediately became a dragon in fulfillment of her vow. Later, when Uisang was building the Pusoksa Temple, a group of ruffians came to disrupt the workers, and the dragon appeared to drive them away, in the form of a giant hovering rock. This is how the temple came to be called Pusoksa, which literally means 'floating stone'.

Having built the Pusoksa Temple, Master Uisang began to propagate the new Flower Ornament Buddhism (*Hwaom* in Korean, *Hua-yen* in Chinese, *Kegon* in Japanese), which stressed the need to put teachings into practice, rather than stop at mere knowledge. While his philosophy was grounded in Flower Ornament Buddhism, it also embraced the Avalokitesvara (Kuanum) Buddhism[2] and the Pure Land doctrines[3].

In a society based on a rigid caste system, Uisang stressed the equality of human beings and did what he could to lessen the suffering of the general public. When King Munmu (reign. 661-681) offered to reward him with land and

---

[2] Bodhisattva (Posal in Korean) is a Sanskrit word, literally meaning 'enlightened being', and refers to one who has reached a high level of enlightenment but has postponed entering eternal nirvana in order to guide others to salvation. Avalokitesvara (Kuanum in Korean) is the Bodhisattva of compassion, and the most widely revered among all the Bodhisattvas. He is believed to have 1,000 arms and 1,000 eyes, in order to see anyone who calls for his help, and save them from disaster.

[3] Pure Land is a branch of Buddhism which focuses on Amitabha Buddha, who is believed to preside over the Pure Land. Followers believe that chanting Amitabha Buddha's name in the current life will lead them to reborn in the Pure Land, or in other words, to escape samsara, the cycle of repeated birth and death. The simplicity of this form of practice has contributed greatly to its popularity throughout East Asia.

servants, Uisang politely refused, insisting that everyone is equal before the Dharma, and a Buddhist practitioner cannot have servants. When the king later began the construction of a castle at Kyongju, Uisang urged him to stop, saying, "If a king rules wisely, the simple drawing of a line in the earth will be a fortification that none will dare cross, and it will avert disasters. But if he rules unwisely, even the Great Wall of China will not be enough to keep misfortunes out". In this way, Uisang's influence extended beyond the Buddhist community into all corners of society.

In his *Hwaom Ilsung Popgyedo* (Diagram of Dharma-realm of Single Vehicle of Flower Ornament Buddhism), Uisang distilled the core teachings of Flower Ornament Buddhism, which he taught and practiced. Although he passed away at the age of 78 in 702 AD, his ten foremost disciples subsequently strove to propagate the teachings of their master, and Uisang posthumously became the founder of the Korean Flower Ornament School. Even though Uisang did not go to Japan, he gained a considerable following among Japanese Buddhists. In 1219 A.D., a multi-paneled scroll called the Kegon Emaki (now at Kozan-ji in Kyoto) was painted, documenting the adventures of Uisang on his trip to China.

Wonhyo had many distinguished disciples, but organized his followers in a different way to Master Uisang. Rather than spreading the Dharma by means of an organized sect, Wonhyo chose to interact directly with the public. In order to sow the seeds of Buddhism in people's hearts, he visited countless hamlets and villages all over the country. Uisang, on the other hand, remained in his residence on Mount Taebaek, and focused his efforts on training disciples.

Wonhyo showed an interest in Taoism and even medical science, but Uisang never ventured outside Buddhism. Uisang maintained the appearance of a strict practitioner, while Wonhyo walked the streets in the guise of a commoner.

Although Wonhyo and Uisang had different backgrounds and approaches to living, their sincere wish to follow the spiritual path, and to illuminate people's minds with Buddha's Dharma, were precisely the same. These two men represent contrasting archetypes of intellectual pioneers in ancient Korea. One dedicated his entire life to serious scholarship, and the other immersed himself in the everyday world, and practiced the 'Great Compassion'. Both, however, were engaged in a tireless endeavor to open the gates of the human mind.

2. A Journey to the Tang

The publication of the new translations of Master Xuanzang signaled a time of great change for Buddhism. In terms of intellectual maturity, the Buddhist tradition of 7th century China had reached its zenith. Many learned monks participated in Xuanzang's project to translate the new scriptures, and the study of 'New Buddhism' rapidly became popular. It did not take long for the new translations to reach Korea.

In 650, five years after Xuanzang returned from his studies in India, Wonhyo and Uisang (aged 34 and 26 respectively) embarked on a journey to study in Tang China. At the time, it was common to make the journey by sea. The sea-route passed through Liadong in Koguryo, which bordered with China. Liaodong was a key transport link between China and the Korean peninsula. In the year 650, it was also a place of heightened tension due to a recent invasion by the Tang forces. Because of this, the two practitioners from Silla were wrongly identified as spies by a Koguryo patrol, as they attempted to cross the border. Attempts at espionage were common, and spies often traveled in the guise of itinerant monks. Moreover, Silla and Tang China were allies, whereas Silla and Koguryo were opposed to one another.

Wonhyo and Uisang were apprehended at Liaodong and detained for several weeks. Finally attaining their release, they made their way back to Silla with great hardship, frustrated in their hopes of studying abroad. For Wonhyo, although his journey was ultimately fruitless, his vivid experiences of witnessing ruthless acts of war must have helped greatly to enrich his understanding of life, and assisted in the development of his philosophy.

3. Drinking Water from a Skull

Wonhyo made a second attempt to study in the Tang in the year he turned 44 (661 A.D.), again in the company of Master Uisang. In order to cross the sea to Tang China, they traveled westward. By the time they reached the harbor of the Tanghang castle, darkness had already fallen. Met with strong winds and heavy rain, they were forced to spend the night in an underground shelter. When they awoke the next morning, they realized they had in fact spent the night in a burial chamber. The heavy rain continued, and they were compelled to spend a second night there. During that night, Wonhyo was unable to sleep, kept awake by terrifying sounds and visions of ghosts. This occasion served as an opportunity for a great awakening in the young master.

On the previous night, his mind had been at ease because he thought he was sleeping inside a harmless shelter. On the second night, however, because he knew he was sleeping inside a place of death and burial, he felt very uncomfortable. From this experience, he realised, "When a thought arises, all dharmas (phenomena) arise, and when a thought disappears, the shelter and the tomb are as one".

> The Three Worlds are simply the mind,
> All phenomena are mere perception.
> There being no Dharma outside the mind,
> What else is there to seek?
> I shall not go to the Tang.

Uttering these later story, Wonhyo returned to Silla. He had been awakened to a great Truth, that the Dharma does not exist outside the mind. Truth is not something that one can seek outside oneself, but is an inner realization. Wonhyo perceived the essence of the mind that resides within the inner-self of a human being. This realization of Master Wonhyo became famous in later years, and was re-conceived in the more famous version of the tale.

According to the story, Wonhyo felt very thirsty during the night, and in the darkness began to search for water. He was able to discern an object that looked like a gourd. He picked it up, and found that there was water inside. He tasted it, and it was very sweet. He drank the contents in one gulp, and having satisfied his thirst, slept soundly until dawn. The next morning, when he awoke, he remembered what had occurred and looked for the gourd. The gourd, however, was nowhere to be seen, and he saw only human skulls littering the ground. The gourd had in fact been one of these skulls, and the sweet-tasting water rain which had collected inside. Examining the inside of one of the skulls, he saw that the water was alive with maggots. The profound realization he attained through this experience brought to his mind a Dharma Lecture he had read in the text *Awakening of Faith*.

> When a thought arises, all manner of different minds arise,
> When a thought disappears, all these diverse minds disappear.
> As the Tathagata said, all the Three Worlds are illusion,
> All is a mere fabrication of the mind.

Wonhyo realized that every image and phenomenon comes about as a result of discrimination within the mind, and nothing else. He turned to Uisang and said,

"Did you see me suffering from thirst last night? "

"I saw you in great pain, drinking water from a bowl."

"When I awoke this morning, I saw it was not clean water that I drank, but putrid rainwater gathered within a human skull. When I drank it, it was truly refreshing, and I slept afterwards in great content. After my discovery this morning, I vomited and felt great discomfort. The water this morning is no different from last night. When I did not know what it was, I found it refreshing, but when I found out, I felt discomfort. The dirtiness or the cleanliness of an object does not reside in the object itself, but rather depends on the discrimination within our mind. Now, therefore, I realize that everything is created by the mind. Because I have realized this Truth, I cannot suppress my joy, nor the wish to dance and sing."

Having realized the principle of Mind-Only through this experience, he no longer needed to travel as far as China to seek the Dharma. Having thus attained enlightenment in a single moment, he expressed the state of his mind as follows:

> Because a mind arises, many kinds of dharma come into being.
> When the mind subsides, a sanctuary and a graveyard are one.
> The Three Worlds are simply the mind,
> And all phenomenona are based on consciousness.
> Since there is only the mind, what else is there to seek!

Here 'the mind' refers to karmic hindrance or a discriminative mind. Because discriminations arise, the Dharma exists as a method of eradicating such discriminations. Therefore when all karmic hindrances, or discriminations of the mind, are purified and eradicated, then there is not even the distinction of calmness and anger.

Uisang continued in his journey to the Tang across the sea, as he had originally intended. He studied under the Dharma Master Zhiyan (602-668) for ten years at the Zhixiangsi Temple on Mt. Zhongnan, after which he returned to Silla and propagated Flower Ornament Buddhism widely. In 676 A.D., under a royal prerogative, he built a temple called Pusoksa, and taught many disciples there.

Wonhyo, on his return to Silla, stayed briefly at the Punhwangsa Temple and dedicated himself to study and practice. Using his realizations as a basis for his writings, Wonhyo composed commentaries on the Buddhist scriptures, and his renowned works such as *Kumgang Sammaegyong Non* (Exposition of the Vajrasamadhi Sutra) later served as a guide to countless scholars and practitioners in East Asia. Later, he left the confines of the temple to live amongst the people. He gave them great hope, at times with his words, at times with dancing and singing. His methods of spreading Buddhism were often unconventional, and this was possible because he did not belong to a specific school or sect. Wonhyo was therefore a true pioneer of Buddhism for the ordinary person. Buddhism, he believed, should not be the preserve of an elite group of intellectuals, or used as a tool to reinforce tyrannical power; this was a religion based on formality, or a religion for the nobility. Although a Buddhist, he felt it was necessary to go beyond Buddhism. Because of this, many regard Wonhyo as the master of *muae* (non hindrance), a man who was truly free in every way.

V. Returning to Worldly Life

1. Living with the People

When Buddhism was first introduced to Korea, the emphasis was on form and ceremony. All Buddhist monks strictly observed the monastic rules and precepts. Wonhyo, however, sought to free himself from this rule-based approach that relied on outward constraints.

Not bound by the monastic rules which his fellow monks strictly observed, Wonhyo ate meat with bandits and drank wine with harlots. Many monks and laypersons condemned his acts as immoral. When his fellow monks advised him to keep with the precepts, Wonhyo replied: "Whether a deed is good, or becomes a sin, is difficult to determine. Some actions may appear righteous when the intention behind them is wrong. Likewise, an action may appear dishonorable, but may in some cases have a pure and innocent intention. Whether something is good or bad depends on the mind alone."

Wonhyo's words and deeds were frequently too bizarre for his fellow monks to understand. Sometimes he would stay within the temple and devote himself to practice, without eating or sleeping. At other times he would pass the day with the beggars on the streets. It was only natural that Wonhyo was censured by the Buddhist establishment of the time, which was preoccupied with adherence to rules, and believed that the dignity of a monk should be maintained at all times.

Wonhyo believed that reading the sutra and performing ceremonies within the walls of the temple were not the only way of practicing Buddha's teaching.

Living alongside sentient beings in the outside world, sharing in their sufferings and joys, and passing on the teachings of Buddha to them directly, he felt was a truer way of carrying out Buddha's will. However, few people understood his earnest wish to sow the seeds of Buddhahood in the lowest and least understood levels of society.

Wonhyo went out of his way to visit every part of the country, and to convey the Buddhist teachings in a way that could be easily understood by everyone. Conversing with royal persons and aristocrats, lowly beggars and wayward children, he spread Buddhism far and wide. Due to Wonhyo's efforts, everyone in Silla came to believe in Buddhism. One of the reasons behind its popularity was the new 'Pure Land' doctrine.

According to the Pure Land doctrine, the practitioner should chant "Namu Amitabul" (Praise to Amitabha Buddha) in order to be reborn in a paradise after death. It was a simple but compassionate teaching that ordinary people found attractive and easy to understand, and was as a result far more effective than an abstruse academic theory. Reciting Buddha's name has the effect of calming the mind. In other words, by reciting the mantra or name of Buddha, the mind becomes purified and focused, and thus maintains a continued state of tranquility. Master Wonhyo's teachings concerning the Pure Land spread extensively, and everyone in Silla, both noble and low-born, came to recite Amitabha Buddha's name.

2. An Encounter with Princess Yosok

Wonhyo thought that the true aim of Buddhism was to rescue the minds of sentient beings from suffering. At the time, Buddhism was known only to the aristocracy and the upper classes. Wonhyo began to hold Dharma meetings for groups of ordinary citizens, in order to teach Buddhism to as many people as possible. As greater numbers gathered to listen to Wonhyo's Dharma lectures, his reputation grew, and he became well-known throughout the land.

One day, a beautiful princess attended one of his Dharma lectures, and was greatly impressed by his words. The princess was Yosok, the second daughter of King Muyol (reign. 654-661). Comely and good-natured, as a young girl she was called Ayuta, and was admired by many a Hwarang. Her husband was a Hwarang named Kojin, who had died in the war with Paekche. After listening Wonhyo's teachings, her spirit was greatly shaken.

> Buddha attained enlightenment
> In order to cleanse the suffering of the people
> And to give them happiness.
> This is called Buddha's compassion
> And this is the mindset of the Buddha
> To love all people equally.

For days afterwards, the master's words remained in the mind of the princess. At last, she fell sick with love. Hearing of her illness, the king summoned a famous doctor, but he could find no cause for her illness. One day, the princess said to her maidservant.

"I wish I could behold the Master again, even once."

After much thought, the maid replied,

"Well, your highness! Send a message that you wish to attend the Master's meeting, and hold the meeting at the palace."

The royal family and aristocrats of Silla were devout Buddhists, and would often invite renowned Buddhist teachers to their houses. Wonhyo, who taught regardless of rank, willingly accepted the invitation, and went to the royal palace in a carriage. When he arrived, he delivered the following lecture.

"Everyone possesses the nature of Buddha. Whosoever awakens his mind to learn and practice Buddha's teachings, and walks the path, he or she is a Bodhisattva.[4] In order to become a Bodhisattva, you must strive to escape from the chains of delusion, and share what you have gained freely with all sentient beings. If you practice this constantly, you will attain Buddhahood."

As he was about to return to Punhwangsa Temple after the lecture, a maid came to him and addressed him with great respect.

"Master, the princess would like to serve you some rare tea which has come from abroad."

Wonhyo was led to the princess, whose room was fragrant with the scent of the tea. The princess served him personally, and he drank.

Finally, the princess was unable to suppress her emotion, and cried out,

"Master, I cannot keep my thoughts from you. For a long time I have been sick with a longing for your presence. If you do not save me, I shall surely die."

Wonhyo was embarrassed, and replied.

"Your highness, I do not understand your words. I am a monk, and worldly love is forbidden to me. I must observe the Buddhist precepts."

"But Master, do not the precepts forbid you to leave me to die?"

Wonhyo thought for a while with his eyes closed, and then spoke again.

"Your highness, the Brahma Net Sutra states that the intentional taking of a life is a grave sin, and to leave another to die is also a great sin as well. If this is your true wish, you must first seek the king's permission."

Wonhyo hurriedly left the palace, and for the next few days, prayed and

---

[4] The term *Bodhisattva* was used by the Buddha in the Pali canon to refer to himself both in previous lifetimes and as a young man in his current life, prior to becoming fully enlightened. During his discourses, he recounts his experiences as a young aspirant with the phrase, "When I was an unenlightened Bodhisattva..." The term therefore denotes a being who is heading towards enlightenment, or in other words, a person who practices to attain full enlightenment. In the Mahayana Buddhism of East Asia, a bodhisattva is a saint who already has attained a high degree of enlightenment, and seeks to use his or her wisdom to help sentient beings become liberated from suffering.

meditated to find a way of saving the princess's life. It occurred to him that although a monk is obliged to observe the precepts, there are situations in which it is impossible to follow the rules exactly. Agreeing to the princess's wish, he thought, in order to save her life, was a way of practicing compassion, and a pardonable sin.

After a few days, Wonhyo appeared before the king's palace, singing a song.

Who will lend me an axe that has lost its handle?
I will cut down a beam that will serve as a pillar in Heaven.

Wonhyo sang this song repeatedly, like a madman, and then returned to Punhwangsa Temple at dusk. He continued like this for many days, coming to the palace and then returning again. His strange behaviour became the subject of much discussion, but no one guessed the true meaning of his song. At last, King Muyol came to hear of it. After considering the words of the song, he realized their meaning. An axe that has lost its handle is like a woman who has lost her husband, and a pillar of the Heavens represents an heir to a kingdom.

"Master Wonhyo intends to marry a princess and beget a wise son by her."

The King smiled and thought of his daughter Princess Yosok. He told his officials to conduct Wonhyo secretly to the residence of the princess. Realizing the king's intention to find him, Wonhyo cast himself into a stream. The king's officials carried him, his clothes still wet, to the palace.

After a short time, the princess appeared in a beautiful gown. She approached Wonhyo and poured him a glass of wine. After drinking the wine, he poured a glass for the princess. With this simple ceremony, their marriage was complete.

The intervening days passed as if in a dream. Half a month later, Wonhyo arrived at the princess's palace. Unable to endure the qualms of conscience any longer, he made a firm resolution to return to his original path.

"Princess, today I must leave you. Practice the path of the Bodhisattva, as you heard me bid you at the Dharma meeting in this very palace. Seek the Buddha-nature within and perform many virtuous deeds. Thus you will forget the sorrow of our parting and become a Bodhisattva. I must fulfill my task to teach more people the truth of Buddha, and help them towards enlightenment."

The eyes of the Princess filled with tears.

"Will I ever see you again?"

"Princess, please seek your Buddha-mind, not me. I hope to see you again in the Pure-Land of Happiness."

Wonhyo bowed, his hands folded in prayer, and left the palace.

A few months later, the princess realized that she was pregnant with a child.

"I have conceived the master's child. He has given me another precious karmic tie[5]."

3. Princess Yosok and Solchong

Princess Yosok gave birth to a fine looking boy called Solchong, who later became a distinguished scholar. His official post in government was *Hallim,* serving as counsel to the king and as a drafter of royal decrees. His most famous legacy is the *idu,* a writing system that introduced special characters to accommodate the phonology, syntax and other linguistic features unique to the Korean language within the Chinese script. He is today recognized as one of the Ten Great Sages of Silla.

Although Wonhyo lived apart from his wife and child, it was not in the spirit

---

[5] In Buddhism, human relations are not viewed as accidental, but the result of a connection made in the past. Relationships are formed because two people are meant to meet each other. Thus, the princess is glad that she has been bound closer to the master by the creation of a stronger karmic link through their son.

of abandonment that he left them, nor was he a heartless and irresponsible man who used his Buddhist practice as an excuse to avoid the obligations of human affection and worldly duty. It is recorded that he often resided at the Hyol Temple, where he later entered Nirvana. Given that Solchong's house is said to have been near this temple, it is likely that the three members of Wonhyo's family remained in contact with one another.

When Wonhyo died, Solchong mixed his father's ashes with earth to make a small figurine in his father's likeness. He enshrined the statue at the Pumhwangsa Temple, and went there regularly to pay his respects with great reverence, love and sorrow. One day, as he bowed before the statue of Wonhyo, the statue turned its head towards him. It is said that this is why the statue has its head turned to one side today.

Until the creation of Hangul by King Sejong in the 15th century, Koreans used Hanja, or Chinese script, in their writing. Solchong tried to preserve the national identity of Korea by drawing together the elements of Korea's indigenous speech and using them himself. In a discussion of the three distinguished literary figures of the Silla Kingdom (Kang Su, Choi Chiwon and Solchong), the *Memorabilia of the Three Kingdoms* refers to Solchong as one who "read the Four Books and Five Classics and educated subsequent generations in our native language". The spirit of Solchong lived on after his death, and reached its full realisation in the Korean alphabet (Hangul) of King Sejong.

The sole remaining example of Solchong's writing is an account of a conversation between himself and King Sinmun. Its title is *Hwawanggye* (A Cautionary Tale for the Flower King).

A long time ago, when the Flower King first arrived, he settled on a hill and blossomed into a beautiful tree peony in spring. Because his appearance was so exceptional, flowers from near and far came to pay their respects. One of them was the Rose. "My Lord, I tread upon sand that is as white as snow, and I look out over a sea that is as clear as a mirror. I bathe in the spring rain, and refresh myself in the blameless winds. I live according to my pleasure, and my name is Rose. I have heard of your Majesty's virtues, and desire to share your couch in a fragrant tent. Please accept me my Lord!" Next there appeared a grey-haired old man. His hempen clothes were tightly tied round his waist, and he was barely able to support himself with his walking staff. "My Lord, my name is Pasqueflower. I live by the mountain road, with the faraway fields below, and the tall hills and their lofty peaks above. Your Majesty, even though you possess all you require, I offer you this service. To ensure that you are replete with good food, that your spirit is purified with fine tea and wine, and to minister effective medicine, so that your body is filled with vigor, and every malign influence removed. It is said that even when one has threads of silk and linen, one should not discard the dry grass and reeds, for there will come a time when the silk and linen have run out. Will you do this, Your Majesty?" The Flower King deliberated, "I have seen two flowers – and must accept one and reject the other. The words of Pasqueflower are full of truth, but the beauty of the Rose is rare indeed. It is a hard choice to make." Having heard the king's words, the Pasqueflower spoke again. "I no longer believe Your Highness to be wise and familiar with the ways of the world. In general, if a king does not associate with those who flatter or beguile him, he will live a virtuous and upright life." The Peony, the King of Flowers, then said, "I have erred greatly."

The story is apparently a satire of the then monarch of Silla, King Sinmun, and is found in the *Samguk Yusa* (Memorabilia of the Three Kingdoms), in the section entitled 'Biographies of Solchong'. Solchong continued to be revered after his death, and was awarded the posthumous title of Hongyuhu (Great Confucian Scholar) by King Hyongjong of Koryo in 1022. Together with Choi Chiwon, he was honored in the Confucian shrine as one of the Two Sages of Silla, and a national ceremony at the Great Western Mountain School of Confucianism in Kyongju has been held in his memory ever since.

4. Layman Sosong

After breaking his vow of celibacy and becoming the father of Solchong, Wonhyo acknowledged his new status as a layperson and called himself 'Layman Sosong' or 'Layman Poksong'. 'Layperson' in Buddhism refers to someone who believes, but does not practice as a monk in a temple. 'Sosong' and 'Poksong' are both words which mean a humble person who is lower than anyone else. Layman Sosong could be found in the streets of Silla, visiting taverns and drinking with the men, or joining in games with the children. Weaving an entertaining story, he would deliver the teachings of Buddha as a narrative. Children would run up to him to ask who Buddha was, and mountain outcasts would leave his presence having understood in their hearts something of the Buddha's teaching. In this work, Wonhyo found great joy.

One day, as he was walking, Wonhyo came across a pair of acrobats performing by the roadside. One was walking a tightrope, while the other was below, wearing a mask and holding a small gourd in his hand, dancing to the rhythm of the music. Crowds gathered on all sides to see the performance, and in their excitement began to join in, dancing and clapping. Seeing this, an idea occurred to Wonhyo.

He decided that he should make Buddha's teachings into a song, and teach it to everyone. Taking the phrase "When one is unhindered in all things, one is freed from the cycle of birth and death", he composed a song called "*Muae*" (non-hindrance), and began to teach it to many people. Eventually, children followed him in crowds, singing the Song of Non-hindrance together with him.

The phrase on which the song was based comes from the Flower Ornament Sutra. In the words of the song, Master Wonhyo distilled the meaning of the original phrase in terms that could be understood easily. When a person has cultivated the mind, because he or she has no discriminative thoughts, each and every task is approached with wisdom and equanimity. When the mind has become free in this way, one is liberated from the unending cycle of rebirth. To be unhindered means, in other words, to have no grudges, ill feelings or other obstacles or hindrances in one's mind, and therefore to treat everything and everyone wisely and fairly. In a mind that is truly free and liberated, no feelings of regret or guilt remain. Singing this Song of Non-hindrance, Master Wonhyo traveled from village to village, never staying long in a single place, wandering through every part of the country.

> All sentient beings, listen!
> Listen to Lord Buddha's words!
> Good and bad depend on the mind,
> Clean and unclean depend on the mind.
> If the mind is compassionate and benevolent
> Like the mind of Lord Buddha,
> All shall enter the Land of Happiness!

Making Buddha's teachings accessible to everyone, the song became known in every village Master Wonhyo visited. Moreover, as people gathered to build temples and pagodas, it helped to foster a sense of harmony and cooperation among the citizens of Silla.

VI. Anecdotes from Wonhyo's Life

Numerous tales and anecdotes about the life of Master Wonhyo exist, and often contain elements which appear fantastical or fictitious. For those unfamiliar with the East Asian tradition, it is important to be aware that these elements are there to serve the message of the story, and not to serve as the message itself.

1. Oeosa Temple ('My Fish' Temple)

'Oeosa', which literally means 'My Fish', is an unusual name for a temple. It was here that masters Chajang, Wonhyo, Hyegong and Uisang, who were known as the 'Four Saints of Silla', resided and practiced together. In particular, it is the place of a much-repeated story involving Wonhyo and Hyegong.

The temple was founded by Master Chajang under King Chinpyong (r. 579-632). Originally, it was called Hangsasa. Before Wonhyo made his second attempt to go to Tang China, he built a small monastery in the valley of Mt. Unje, where he practiced day and night. Hyegong was residing at the Hangsasa Temple, where he was teaching 70 students.

One day, the two men were reciting Buddha's name together in the valley of Mt. Unje. Both were seated upon a rock in the lotus position. Suddenly, Hyegong turned to Wonhyo.

"If you are to receive confirmation of enlightenment in China, you must demonstrate supernatural powers. Only then will you prove yourself capable of continuing the lineage of Buddha's Great Dharma. Let us see if you possess such Dharma Power."

The valley was as fresh and unspoilt as a polished mirror, and mountain fish were plentiful in the stream below. It was decided that the two masters would each attempt to catch a fish and swallow it whole. They would then stand upon a rock and both empty their bowels, and if the fish came out alive, this would be a sign that the master had proven his power. Rolling up their sleeves, they both made their way into the stream, and each managed to get hold of a fish. Of the two fish, only one came out alive, and having returned to the water, began to swim vigorously upstream away from the two gentlemen, each of whom claimed that the fish was his own. According to Iryon (1206-1289), the monk who wrote the famous *Samguk Yusa* (Memorabilia of the Three Kingdoms), this is how the temple came to be named 'Oeosa' or 'My Fish'.

2. Master Tae-an and the Raccoon Cubs

Wonhyo did not have a regular teacher, but studied under many masters. One of his teachers was Master Tae-an. One day, Tae-an found some raccoon cubs that had lost their mother, and to save them he went to the town's public well to beg for some milk from the women there. The women, deeply moved by the master's precious Dharma lecture, happily donated some milk.

Master Tae-an carried the milk in a bowl, and climbed over a steep hill until he finally reached the cave where the young cubs were eagerly waiting for their food. Feeling pity for the cubs, he fed and raised them for many days with much compassion.

When the cubs had grown enough for their eyes to shine, Master Wonhyo came to visit him. Master Tae-an asked Master Wonhyo to take care of the cubs for a few days, as he had some urgent business to attend to elsewhere.

Master Wonhyo raised them with great care, but two of them died. Wonhyo, who claimed to be the foremost Buddhist Master in Silla, could not face Tae-an again. Master Wonhyo thought to himself, "Master Tae-an raised the cubs for fifteen days since they were just tiny pieces of flesh and blood, but because of my own thick karmic hindrances and lack of wisdom, I have caused their death". He deeply repented and took the opportunity to awaken his devotion again.

When Master Tae-an returned, he consoled Wonhyo, "There was no way you could have held on to those whose karmic ties were ceasing". A crow was cawing noisily in front of Wonhyo, who could not say anything. Then Master Tae-an said, "Let us fill the crow's stomach and let the raccoons perform a virtuous act," and threw the dead raccoon cubs to the sky. The crow circling above them sensed his luck, and snatched them away as quick as lightening.

3. Saving a Thousand Monks from Death

Once, Master Wonhyo was staying at the Taegosa Temple. As he was about to begin his evening meal, he saw with his wisdom-eye that a large, ageing temple in China was about to collapse.

Meanwhile, at the temple in China, the thousand resident student-monks[6] were about to eat their dinner, unaware that they were in danger of being crushed to death. At that moment, Wonhyo quickly removed the plates from his dining table, and hurled the table towards the temple in China.

The monks' supper was interrupted when a strange object appeared in the sky and began to circle above the temple courtyard. The kitchen monk saw it first and alerted his fellow practitioners. The monks stopped eating, astonished by the

_____

[6] Novice monks who focused on studying the Sutras, before progressing to the practice of meditation.

remarkable sight, and poured into the yard. The object began to make its way slowly towards the forest outside the temple, as if beckoning the monks forward. When the thousand monks had all emerged from the temple grounds, the temple suddenly collapsed behind them. The monks turned, and saw in disbelief the place where they had been recently in ruins. It had all happened in a matter of moments.

The object fell from the sky into a field, and the monks pressed around it. The object was a wooden table, and on it was written 'This table from Wonhyo in the East to save his fellow monks'. Finally realizing what had happened, they all folded their hands and bowed with reverence towards Silla in the East. As they continued to give thanks and express their respect, the table rose again into the empty sky, and began to move slowly eastwards. The monks followed it, and having boarded a ship, crossed the Yellow Sea to seek Master Wonhyo in Silla.

Wonhyo was staying at Chokpanam Monastery, which was part of the Changansa Temple. He was surprised to find a thousand monks suddenly requesting an audience with him. As the monastery was too small to accommodate a thousand people, Wonhyo arranged temporary residences for them at Changansa, and searched for a place where the thousand monks could be housed permanently. Finally, he built a large temple on the site of the current day Wunhungsa, which was large enough to accommodate the monks. Above the temple was a plain where he taught the monks and schooled them in the teachings of the Flower Ornament Sutra. For this reason, the mountain is called Mt. Chonsong (Thousand Saints Mountain), and the stretch of land is called Hwaom (Flower Ornament Plain).

Although this tale is extraordinary, at the very least we can infer that a considerable number of Chinese monks studied under Wonhyo, and that the basis of his teaching was the Flower Ornament Sutra. It is a fact that the Chinese Dharma Master Xianshou Fazang, a proponent of the Flower Ornament School, makes frequent references to Master Wonhyo in his writings. Similarly, the author of *Zhengdaoge* (Songs of Enlightening Truth), Master Yongming Yanshou, speaks of the importance of Wonhyo's philosophical writings. At the time, Buddhism was the universal system of values in East Asia, and issues of spirituality were considered even more important than those of nationality. In this story, we see how Wonhyo's influence extended beyond the borders of Silla and was felt widely throughout China.

4. Flower Ornament Plains

In South Kyongsang Province, there is an area near the Naewonsa Temple that is called the Flower Ornament Plain, where the events of this story are believed to have occurred. The thousand monks of Master Wonhyo who resided on this plain were in the habit of begging for food and alms from those living nearby. As the monks were so numerous, Wonhyo soon realized that they were becoming a burden on the villages in the area. This troubled him greatly, and he pondered as to how this problem might be solved.

One day, he told the monks, "As of today, no practitioner may beg for alms. Do not seek meals from another." Wondering at what their master might mean by this, the monks grew anxious that they would starve to death.

Master Wonhyo privately summoned one of the monks, and said to him, "Do exactly as I tell you. If you go down to the village, you will find a very wealthy household. Take an empty sack to the house and ask the owner to fill it with rice. Do not return until the sack is full. Be sure to see that it is done properly!"

Following his master's instructions, the monk went down to the house with an empty sack. He beat his wooden gong and recited Buddha's name, and the house owner, hearing him, went to fetch a measure of rice. He poured the measure into the sack the monk was holding, and it became full.

The monk began to tie the neck of the sack, and the owner turned away, thinking that the monk would now leave. The monk, however, realized that the sack had somehow become empty, and not a single grain of rice remained. Puzzled, and remembering his master's instructions not to return until the sack was full, he beat the gong once again and recited Buddha's name. The owner thought this strange.

"I have given you a sackful," he said, "If I give you more, how will you carry it? It will be too heavy for you."

But when he looked at the sack, he saw that it was empty, and the rice he had poured in moments ago was no longer there. Murmuring that this was something even evil spirits would marvel at, he went to fetch another measure of rice. Having filled the sack, he turned away again. The sack became empty once again, however, and even when it was filled a third time, the same thing happened.

At last, the owner realized the truth. 'I have heard', he thought to himself, 'that the enlightened master Wonhyo is staying on the mountain. He must be the one who is making the rice vanish like this. If I had not realized this, then who knows, all the grain I have stored up might suddenly disappear in the middle of the night, and reappear in the storehouse at the temple! Then not only would I lose my rice and become a beggar, but I would not even have performed the virtuous act of giving away my wealth. Since this is the case, I will simply offer up my rice to the temple, and do a good deed'. He then addressed the monk, "Monk, I understand your master's wishes. Please go back to the temple".

"I cannot go back, sir. My master told me not to return until the sack was full."

"Very well. I will fill the sack again, if you promise to tell your Master that I will bring a hundred bags of rice to the temple tomorrow."

With these words, he poured another measure of rice into the sack, and this time it remained full. The monk then returned to the temple, and reported to his master what had happened.

"Master, I had a very strange experience today."

"What was it?"

The monk then told his master how the rice had disappeared three times, and that the sack had been filled the fourth time. He continued, "I cannot understand it, nor can I fully believe it. The wealthy man said he knew it was the work of Master Wonhyo's dharma power, and promised to bring a hundred bags of rice as an offering tomorrow".

Wonhyo smiled and said, "I suspected he might".

On the next day, when the wealthy man came to the temple with the rice, the road to the temple was filled with other men laden with offerings. When the rumor of the previous day's events had spread, the other wealthy men in the neighborhood had all thought to themselves, 'If I sit here and do nothing like a fool, I will not escape the power of the Master. I should make my offering as quickly as I can'. Thus, everyone rushed to bring their offerings of food. As a result, the temple storehouse was filled even though none of the monks had gone out to beg for alms. According to the story, the thousand monks of Master Wonhyo never again suffered from lack of food.

5. Kwangdok and Omjang

During the reign of King Munmu, there were two men called Kwangdok and Omjang. Kwangdok lived with his wife in a village to the west of the Punhwangsa Temple, and made his living weaving straw-shoes. Omjang stayed at a hermitage at Namak, and lived by fire-fallow farming. They were both diligent in reciting Amitabha Buddha's name, and made a pact that whichever of them should enter the Western Pure Land first, he would send a message to the other.

One day, as the sun was setting and the shadows were growing longer, Omjang heard a sound outside his window. He realized it was the voice of his friend Kwangdok.

"I am going to the Pure Land, my brother. Be faithful to Buddha, stay here for as long as you must, but follow me as quickly as you can!"

When Omjang opened the door and went outside, he heard beautiful music echoing through the clouds.

The next day, when he visited his friend's house, he found that Kwangdok had indeed passed away. Together with the man's wife, he searched for a suitable place to bury him, and after the funeral service was complete, he said to her, "Since your husband has passed away, let me lodge at your house". Kwangdok's wife agreed, and from then on the two lived in the same house.

One night, Omjang came to Kwangdok's wife and attempted to embrace her. Startled, she said to him, "Dharma Master, your search for the Pure Land is like a man in a tree who looks for a fish." Taken aback by her words, he asked, "Kwangdok lived as your husband, and he has entered the Pure Land. Why should I not follow him?" Kwangdok's wife replied, "It is just as I have said. Your search for the Western Pure Land is like a man who looks for a fish in the branches of a tree. My husband lived with me for more than ten years, but he never shared my bed or embraced me with an impure heart. Every night he sat on the floor and prayed reciting Amitabha Buddha's name. It is written that when a man walks a thousand miles, his first step reveals his destination. Seeing how you practice, I believe you can journey to the East, but not the West."

Much ashamed, Omjang departed. Going before Master Wonhyo, he entreated him sincerely to show him the path that he should tread. Having pity, the master taught him the Dharma of the Observing the Mind. From this point onward, Omjang kept his body pure, repented deeply for his sins, and devoted himself solely to practicing the Dharma. In time, he also entered the Western Pure Land. There he discovered that Kwangdok's wife, who was a servant at the Punhwangsa Temple during her lifetime, was in fact one of incarnations of Boddhisattva Kuanum.

If we consider the people in this tale – Kwangdok, who weaved straw-shoes, Omjang, a fire-fallow farmer, and Kwangdok's wife, a servant at the Punhwangsa Temple – we can see that Wonhyo's mission to spread knowledge of Buddhism had succeeded among ordinary people as well as in the higher levels of society. Moreover, it shows that the practice of Buddhism was not seen as the sole province of monks. Laypersons of every kind put Buddhist teachings into practice in their daily lives. The reason for the widespread popularity of the Pure Land concept must have been its simplicity and fundamental attractiveness. Another thing this tale illustrates is that everyone is equally endowed with Buddha-Nature, irrespective of class, position or wealth. Even if one does not understand the complex Buddhist scriptures, if one truly devotes oneself to one of the several methods of practice appropriate to one's particular level, anyone can uncover their Buddha-Nature.

6. Wonhyo Declines an Offering from the Heavens

Once, when Master Uisang was residing at the Hongryonam Monastery of Naksansa, and Master Wonhyo was staying at the Yonghyolsa Temple on Mt. Sorak, Uisang invited Wonhyo to visit him. To Wonhyo's surprise, when midday arrived, no meal was served at the temple. When he enquired as to the reason for this, Uisang explained to Wonhyo that there was no source of water at the monastery. As they were unable to cook rice, they relied on offerings of meals which were brought down to them from the Heavens by a divine being. The hours continued to pass, however, and even at four in the afternoon, the heavenly offering still had not come.

Wonhyo arose from where he was sitting, and said, "It is not proper that heavenly meals should be received in the world of sentient beings, even for the benefit of those who are greatly enlightened". He took a cane, and drove it into a rock behind the monastery to create a new spring.

When Wonhyo had left the temple grounds, the heavenly being appeared with the usual offering of food. Uisang asked why the meal had arrived so late in the day. The divine being explained that while Master Wonhyo had been present, the guardian devas of the Flower Ornament Order were surrounding the area, and it did not dare to enter. When Master Wonhyo departed, the devas departed together with him, and it was possible to approach the temple.

This story shows that Uisang was a great enlightened master who received offerings from heavenly beings. At the same time, it shows that Wonhyo's enlightenment was greater than that of Master Uisang, and also that Wonhyo was the foremost exponent of the Flower Ornament Sutra. Wonhyo's statement that it was not right for offerings of heavenly meals to be received in the world of sentient beings reveals the extreme humility with which he approached his life and study.

7. Master Wonhyo's Masterpiece: Exposition of the Vajrasamadhi Sutra

The queen of Silla once developed a brain tumor, and neither famous doctors nor renowned shamen were able to heal her. A sage at the court declared that the queen's condition could only be cured by medicine obtained from abroad. The king dispatched one of his trusted courtiers to China in order to find the medicine.

The courtier boarded a ship, and began to make his way to the Tang. While he was at sea, an aged man appeared to him, and spoke these words, "In order to cure the queen's illness, you must come with me to the Dragon Palace. There, you must speak with the Dragon King. Only then will you obtain the remedy".

The old man led the courtier into the depths of the sea, and before long he was standing before the throne of the Dragon King.

The Dragon King asked the courtier where he had come from.

"Your Highness, I am sent from Silla. Before I was brought here, I was on a journey to the Tang to seek medicine for our Queen's illness."

"You were well advised to come here", the Dragon King replied, "for your queen will soon recover."

"What medicine can cure her?"

"Not medicine, but another means will save the queen. Her karmic tie with Buddha is strong, and her illness will be cured through doing Buddha-work."

"What Buddha-work is that, Your Highness?"

"In this Palace, there is a sutra called the Adamantine Scripture, which has not yet been revealed to the world. Take this sutra and see that it becomes known to all. If this is done, the Queen will make a full recovery. Guard it, and make haste!"

The Dragon King then gave him a bundle of leaves on which the sutra was written. To ensure their safety, he opened the man's leg and placed the sutra inside it. He then closed the wound, and gave the courtier a jar of ointment. "When you return to your country, remove the sutra and apply this ointment to the wound. Your leg will then be healed."

The Dragon King continued, "Be sure that Master Tae-an is the one who puts the leaves in order and binds them. See that Master Wonhyo composes a commentary and delivers a Dharma Lecture on the new scripture. If you do this, the queen is certain to be cured."

The Dragon King carried him to the surface, and sent him on his way. When the courtier returned, the king of Silla was overjoyed, and immediately sent out a command that the holy man Tae-an should be brought to the palace. However, no-one had heard of Tae-an, and there was great anxiety in the court.

One day, a strange monk appeared in the kingdom dressed in outlandish garments. Beating an alms bowl made of copper, he wandered from place to place, crying "Tae-an! Tae-an!". Thinking that this monk was perhaps the holy man who would bind the sutra, the courtier who had brought back the message from the Dragon King went to the monk and requested to speak with him. He told him the story of his visit to the Dragon Palace, and the monk agreed to accompany him to the Royal Court. Master Tae-an had at last been found.

Outside the palace, the monk said to the courtier, "There is no need for me to enter a worldly palace. Bring the sutra out to me". When he was brought the loose leafs, Tae-an quickly arranged them into six chapters, and the meaning of the text could finally be understood. However, as he handed the sutra to the courtier, he said, "Only Master Wonhyo has the wisdom to compose the commentary on this sutra. You must seek him out". And the monk went on his way, singing his wonted song.

Meanwhile, Master Wonhyo was studying at Sangju, his birthplace. A messenger was dispatched to convey him the sutra, and Wonhyo, aware that he was coming, went out to meet him on an ox. The messenger respectfully handed him the sutra, and Wonhyo quickly glanced through the pages. He then placed an inkstone between the horns of the ox, picked up his brush, and began to compose his commentary there and then. Before the ox reached the capital city Kyongju, he had completed a five-volume commentary. This commentary is now also referred to as the 'Horn Vehicle', as it was written while riding an ox, and is a sutra of the Great Vehicle (Mahayana Buddhism).

Shortly afterwards, the king asked Master Wonhyo to give a Dharma Lecture based on the new sutra at the Hwangnyongsa Temple. On the night before, a group of envious plotters stole the commentary he had prepared. Wonhyo postponed the lecture for three days, informing the king as to why. He then wrote a new commentary in three volumes, which in later years was regarded as the writing of a Bodhisattva rather than that of a great master, and referred to as *non* (treatise). It was produced by Wonhyo at the peak of his intellectual powers, and contains several themes common in Wonhyo's work. These themes include the role of meditative absorption (Sanskrit. samadhi), the importance of innate potential for enlightenment (Sanskrit. tathagatagarbha), the inspiration of original enlightenment, and the abandonment of the spurious to appreciate reality.

When the king and queen, government officials, renowned monks and the ordinary subjects were gathered together at the Hwangnyongsa Temple, Master Wonhyo let out his Lion's Roar[7]. When the Dharma Lecture came to end, the crowd remained still for a long time, their minds filled with reverence and joy. Then Wonhyo departed from his place, and said, "A hundred rafters were needed, and yet I was not summoned. The main bulwark is needed, yet I alone am capable".

This statement was referring to the fact that he had not been allowed to attend the Assembly of Hundred Seats, a council of a hundred eminent monks, or 'rafters' according to the metaphor used here. By referring to himself as the 'main bulwark', Wonhyo signified that he alone was needed to provide a solid foundation for Buddhism in Silla. It is important to realize that these words were not spoken out of arrogance or disparagement. By reprimanding the monks who were motivated by success and praise, he thus liberated them from their ignorance and conceit. Hearing Wonhyo's censure, it is said that the assembly of distinguished monks lowered their heads in shame, and repented deeply for their error.

Commentaries on Buddhist scriptures are usually referred to as 'so', which means discourse or discussion. But this commentary of Wonhyo was given the title 'non' which is better translated as 'treatise'. The designation 'non' signifies a work of the highest importance, and that the text forms part of the Great Canon of Scriptures, also known as the Tripitaka. In fact, 'non' is reserved only for the writings of the Buddha and great masters such as Nāgārjuna or Vasubandhu, whose level of enlightenment was similar to that of Buddha. In the history of

---

[7] A Buddhist term designating a powerful form of teaching that subdues karmic hindrances and awakens inner wisdom in the listeners.

East Asian Buddhism, only five men have written works that have been classified as '*non*'. This places Wonhyo very highly indeed among the Sages of East Asia.

VII. Following Buddha's Path

1. A Beacon that Burns Eternally

The fierce conflicts between the Three Kingdoms of Korea ended in the year 686 A.D.. Ten years after the final remnants of the Tang Chinese army had disappeared from the Korean peninsula, Korea was filled with a renewed sense of peace. In this year, Wonhyo's life of vigor and devotion also reached its close. At the age of seventy, on the thirtieth day of the third lunar month, the height of spring, Wonhyo ended his karmic ties with the world at a temple near Hyol in Kyongju. Master Uisang, then in his sixties and teaching Flower Ornament Buddhism at the Pusoksa Temple on Taebaek mountain, is likely to have been present, as well as Wonhyo's 20-year-old son Solchong, who had greatest cause to grieve. However, no record of his passing remains. Upon his tombstone is inscribed, "He strove to master the principles of the universe, and made his goal the most profound Truth of all".

Master Zanning from China, author of *Song Gaoseng Zhuan* (Lives of Eminent Monks Compiled in Song), portrays Wonhyo the scholar in the following terms:

> Wonhyo valiantly assailed the bastion of opinion, fearlessly made his way through the multitude of the scriptures, and with swiftness and resolve, marched ever onward, never retreating. Widely versed in the Threefold Principles of Observance, Clarity and Wisdom, the people

of his country called him a 'Match for Ten Thousand'. Such was his mastery of Truth, such was his holiness.

It is significant that the people of Silla praised him using the terms described above. A 'Match for Ten Thousand' means one who has the wisdom and courage to confront countless enemy troops alone without difficulty. Legendary generals such as Guanyu and Zhangfei were given this title, and it is interesting that Wonhyo, a scholar, was compared to the most capable generals of the day. It is a way of expressing his vigorous and distinctive approach to life, on the battlefield of the Dharma.

For the people of Silla, 'a match for ten thousand' was certainly no exaggeration. In the 1600 year history of Korean Buddhism, his teachings and writings occupy the summit of achievement. No previous master had scaled the heights attained by Wonhyo in his lifetime, and subsequent masters of a similar caliber are few and far between.

The 240 volumes Wonhyo is known to have written, covering almost every aspect of Buddhism, including Hinayana, Mahayana and the Tripitaka of sutras, vinaya and shastras, can only be described as a superhuman effort of study and authorship. The depth of perception and clarity of interpretation that are evident in his key works *Taesung Kisillon So* (Commentary on the Awakening of Faith) and *Kumgang Sammaegyong Non* (Exposition of the Vajrasamadhi Sutra) have received praise from Buddhist masters and scholars across the globe, and remain a beacon of Truth for the Buddhist world.

2. The Aesthetics of the One Mind

Sleeping inside an underground shelter yesterday, I was at ease,
But sleeping inside a tomb last night, my mind was greatly agitated.

Now I understand - when a thought arises, all dharmas (phenomena) arise,
And when a thought disappears, the shelter and the graveyard are one and the same.
The Three Worlds exist simply in the mind,
And all phenomena are mere perception.
Since there is no Dharma outside the mind,
How can it be sought for elsewhere?

In this song, composed after his famous awakening in the underground burial chamber, Wonhyo borrows a phrase from *Awakening of Faith*, a classic introduction to the Mahayana Buddhist tradition, in order to express his radical change in perspective. Taking the phrase:

When a thought arises, all manner of phenomena arise
When the thought disappears, all manner of phenomenon disappear.

He altered it to:

Because one thought arises, all manner of phenomena arise,
Because the mind disappears,
The shelter and the graveyard are no longer separate.

The discovery of the 'One Mind' transformed Wonhyo's life, and he was reborn as a practitioner. The wisdom he acquired through this conversion to the Alaya Consciousness was profound indeed. Once he had realized that the two opposites of purity and defilement become one through this One Mind, there was nothing to hold him back. Unhindered and fully liberated, his subsequent endeavors in writing and spreading Buddha's teachings became true 'Non-Hindrance'.

Viewed through the lens of Alaya Consciousness, Wonhyo realized that the underground shelter and the tomb are the same, and the same is true of the cycle of birth-and-death and Nirvana. Viewing the life of mankind on the basis of Non-Duality, he abandoned his journey abroad and began life afresh in his homeland. Because of this great realization, Wonhyo came to look at the human condition in a fundamentally different way.

'Since the Dharma does not exist outside the mind, where would one go to seek the Dharma? If there is Truth in the Tang, why does it not exist in Silla? Surely the true cultivation of the mind is about the "how" and not the "where"? Surely the question is how to solve the problem of life and death, and not where one should solve it.'

Thus Wonhyo reasoned with himself. Reflecting upon the dramatic change that had occurred in his outlook in the short space of a day and a night, he began to analyze the Ayala Consciousness in greater depth.

The biological conditions of all living beings are the same, and therefore the Truth can be found anywhere. Why then must we journey to the Tang? How are Silla and the Tang different, and how are they the same? What is here? What should be here? How can we lessen the gap between the two? Standing between these two axes of universal truth, he deliberated on these questions, and experienced momentous convulsions of thought.

Through this profound change in his understanding of One Mind, Wonhyo perceived the true nature of the mind that exists within every sentient being. Wonhyo realized that this One Mind is infinite, and at the same time the Mind of all sentient beings. Through this spontaneous self-awakening, he gave up his journey to the Tang, and became a leading visionary and thinker in his own country.

In the *Taesung Kisillon So* (Commentary on the Awakening of Faith), Wonhyo explains the theory of 'One Mind' as follows:

What is One Mind? Because all phenomena of purity and impurity are not separate in nature, and the doors of truth and untruth are likewise the same, it is called 'One'. Where there is no discrimination between the two, all phenomena are at their truest, and are like empty air. Because their nature is naturally understood, it is called 'Mind'. Since there is no such thing as two, there cannot be such a thing as one, and if there is no 'one', what can we call the Mind? Because this Truth defies description and abstract thought, not knowing what words to use, I reluctantly call it 'One Mind'.

'One Mind' lies beyond the horizon of 'the other'. Wonhyo discovered the concept of One Mind outside the constraints of a world of binary alternatives. Because contrasting terms such as clean and unclean depend upon it, One Mind serves as the basis for all existence. When we discover the One Mind, which is the source of everything, discriminating minds do not arise. The division of the Three Kingdoms, the division of East and West, North and South – all melt away in the furnace of the One Mind.

Sentient beings are fundamentally enlightened. Therefore, enlightenment is not attained by acquiring something else. It is because we are swayed by winds of ignorance and waves of desires, that we are unable to see the Truth, and this is the burden we carry as sentient beings. However, by cultivating the mind and by calming the winds of ignorance, like a peaceful ocean, the enlightenment within each person will clearly reveal itself. Truth is distorted if we observe it only for a particular moment, or from a particular perspective.

With the One Mind as his guiding principle, Wonhyo devoted himself to serving Buddha. It was with this One Mind that he produced literary works, and it was with the ever-present goal of the One Mind that he lived his life of 'Non-Hindrance'. By returning to the root of One Mind, he sought to discover his true self, and to benefit all living beings.

3. The Logic and Ethics of Hwajaeng (Harmonizing Disputations)

People's interests are often in conflict, and peaceful days in the world are few. Although everyone seeks peace and reconciliation, yielding to the will and opinion of others is hard.

The 7th century A.D. was a time of great discord in East Asia, and the Korean peninsula was engulfed in war. The constraints of the rigid class system had also created civil unrest. Wonhyo's life was not untouched by this general strife. He was frustrated in his plan to study in the Tang when he was arrested as a spy at Liaodong. Though Wonhyo was originally invited to attend the national 'Assembly of Hundred Seats', his position was undermined by rivals and the invitation was later withdrawn. He also was robbed of his first commentary on the Adamantine Sutra prior to the inaugural Dharma Lecture ordered by the King.

Wonhyo, however, chose a path of reconciliation that embraced discord and conflict. As a way of dealing with such situations, he proposed the method of Hwajaeng. Hwajaeng did not allow for a distinction between positive and negative, but emphasized that everything in the world is interconnected. Due to this interdependency, and the common origin shared by all things, the whole and the part exist as one. Therefore one should not 'wander in the valleys without seeing the mountain' or 'rush towards a forest ignoring the trees'. From one perspective, we are one, and from another, we are many. This thought is summarized in the following passage of Wonhyo.

> Viewed as a whole, there is One Perspective;
> Viewed separately, there are Ten Gates.
> Though viewed separately, the One is not greater in number.
> Though viewed as a whole, Ten are not smaller in number.
> When viewed as many, the Ten are not unwieldy;
> Though viewed alone, the One is not finite.

Like this, Wonhyo was unrestricted in his treatment of the one and the many. Nor was he concerned whether his views were accepted or rejected by others. If there is no attachment to acceptance, there is nothing to gain by affirmation, nor is there anything to lose if one's views are rejected. In an argument, we often ignore the opinions of others, and hold on to our original position. However, whenever we try to understand or propose something whilst attached to our own position or preferences, it is hard for us to view the issue objectively, from a holistic perspective. Thus it is difficult to see an object as it really is. We see the world filtered through our own perspective, we measure things by our own personal standards, and approach matters with ourselves as the central point of reference. All such expressions of arrogance, however, come from the ego.

To avoid distorting reality with a self-centered perspective, we need to be free from preconceptions and prejudices. This means both to humble, and to open, our minds.

As Wonhyo remarked in the *Commentary on the Awakening of Faith*, "If you are free from preconceptions, you and the other person will be equal". In order to measure something with dimensions that exceed the limitations of our own standards, we must be prepared to discard these fixed standards.

Although it is easy to say that we have 'let go' of something, it is in fact very difficult for our mind to truly let go. As long as we cling to ourselves, or believe that others are separate from us, it is impossible for us to empty the mind. A person who tries to stop a fight must be impartial. Hwajaeng is possible only when it based on absolute impartiality. When we are capable of acts that are truly without ego, like the acts of the Buddha, we can finally be freed from differences and disputes between scholars and academics.

If we remain trapped within the narrowness of our own perceptions, and insist on the absolute validity of a certain viewpoint, or dogmatize a given position, problems will inevitably arise. Wonhyo described this attitude as follows: "There are those who put forward their own limited opinion, on the basis of the little they have heard; if others agree, they are pleased, but if others disagree, they say that they are wrong. Like a man who observes the sky through a hole in a reed, such people approve when others view the sky through the same hole, but claim that those who do not are unable to see the sky."

Wonhyo reprimanded the unwise practice of those who, being narrow-minded and weak, maintain that only their opinion is correct and do not accept the words of others. Though standards are not always the same, they are not always different. Nothing is the same, and yet nothing is really different. In the words of Wonhyo: "Because they are many, many ways are possible, and because they are one, all ways are ultimately one, single way. How could there be only one path in life? There is a broad highway, a sea-route, and a solitary footpath. How could we say only one road is right? Any of the paths can lead us to the ultimate goal of happiness. If we open the narrow and constrained mind, an open sky of possibilities is revealed."

The spoken or written word is like a finger that points to the moon. It is enough to look at the moon, rather than simply look at the finger. As Wonhyo said: "With words, I will illustrate the Dharma that is beyond words. Just like the finger that points to the moon, the moon and the finger are not the same."

If one focuses on figures of speech, it is easy to miss the essence of what is being said. Therefore it is better to seek the meaning behind the words, rather than focusing on the words themselves. Looking at words alone, it is difficult to accommodate another's opinion, whatever it might be. But if we look at the meaning of the words, there is nothing that cannot be accommodated.

> With words, there is nothing to accept;
> With meaning, there is nothing to deny.

This is another lesson from Wonhyo. If we lose sight of the meaning, and merely cling to words, it is no different from examining the tip of one's finger, and observing that it is not the moon. It would be better to shed our preconceptions and prejudices, and listen to the words of others. Better still if we were able to look through the eyes of others, and perceive the true unspoken words of the mind.

4. Philosophy of Ilche-Muae (Non-Hindrance in Everything)

The principle of Ilche-Muae formed the basis of Wonhyo's life. Not being attached to any one thing, he was a totally free man. His goal of being 'unhindered' in everything is expressed in the words, "One who has no attachment to anything will immediately be liberated from the cycle of birth and death". He did not see the Buddha and sentient beings as separate, asserting "When we consider it closely, the mind of all sentient beings is undivided and therefore totally without hindrance. It is as tranquil as the empty air, calm like the ocean's surface, and level with no basis of discrimination". Therefore he saw that an inherent, limitless freedom existed in the minds of sentient beings, and that he himself could become a wholly liberated being. Thus he proposed the concepts of 'Single Vehicle' and 'One Mind', without affiliating himself with any particular sect or school.

In terms of his philosophy, he placed most importance on the rediscovery of the One Mind. In terms of day-to-day practice, he considered 'Without-Hindrance' to be the most important. The freedom he aimed at was not based on the desire to escape, but was in order to harness the power of Non-Duality in the earthly world and benefit sentient beings. In other words, he believed the ceaseless practice of compassion and mercy towards all sentient beings was the key to sustaining a life of perfect Non-Hindrance.

Whether in theory or in practice, Wonhyo was truly unhindered in everything. Viewed from his perspective, all beings are free and unhindered, because all are rooted in the One Mind. Owing to the waves of ego which assail us, however, we lose the freedom of our own true will, and so wander amid unending sufferings. Therefore, we must return to our original state, and rediscover the root of our One Mind. Here, we find a parallel with the German philosopher Martin Heidegger's concepts of homelessness and homecoming. Sentient beings are in essence 'homesick', and Buddha is the home they seek. Methods of spiritual practice are simply a means of completing this journey home.

5. Breaking the Brush

While attempting to liberate people from their sufferings in the spirit of the compassionate Bodhisattvas of Mahayana Buddhism, Wonhyo went beyond the meaningless formalities that came with them. At the same time, he stressed the importance of inner awakening within a practitioner, made possible by sincere repentance. *Song Gaoseng Zhuan* (Lives of Eminent Monks Compiled in Song) by Zanning (919-1001) describes Wonhyo's unhindered life as follows:

> His words were forthright and direct, and his behaviour digressed from the accepted norms, often going against what was considered right and proper. In the company of laypersons, he would enter taverns and brothels. Like Zhigong, he carried a knife and an iron staff. Sometimes he would compose commentaries on the Flower Ornament Sutra. At other times he would strike up the Komungo (Korean zither) to enliven the atmosphere of the temple. One night he would dwell at the house of a villager. By day, he might sit in meditation by a stream in the mountains. Like this, Wonhyo practiced and lived in a spontaneous manner, and did not abide by any fixed rules.

Wonhyo's unhindered way of life began after his realization of the One Mind. Spending time with clowns, butchers, prostitutes, aged farmers, and unlettered peasants, he shared in their joys and sorrows, and practiced compassion towards all he met. As he travelled the country singing and dancing, everybody from housekeepers to young children in the streets came to know Buddha's name through his words. Wonhyo had become fully aware of the innate preciousness of all living beings. He tried to bridge the spurious division between the nobles and common people. If Korea was to be unified, it was not enough for the walls of three kingdoms to be broken down and for one monarch to rule the country. True unification could only occur when the walls within people's hearts were broken down, and everyone desired to live together without hate and mistrust. Thus Wonhyo conceived, from a Buddhist perspective, what the true unification of Korea's three kingdoms should be.

While staying at Puhwangsa Temple and writing the *Commentary on Flower Ornament Sutra*, Wonhyo suddenly broke the writing brush he was using, having come to the chapter entitled 'Returning Merit to Others'. This symbolic action was based on a profound insight he received while contemplating the message of the *Flower Ornament Sutra* – namely, that its profound teachings could not be carried out in fullness by mere studying alone. The *Flower Ornament Sutra* taught that one must become a Bodhisattva, resolve to attain enlightenment, and give back one's merit to all sentient beings. He believed that 'giving back one's merit to others' could be achieved by sharing the experience of his own enlightenment with all. However, he realized that the real meaning of the sutra could not be understood through words and letters. So, he left the temple to live the teachings of the sutra fully in the wider world.

VIII. The Contemporary Meaning of Wonhyo's Thought

1. Wonhyo's Spirit, Eternal Present

Wonhyo was more than a renowned Buddhist monk; he was also an inspired philosopher, an accomplished scholar and a prolific writer. He played a significant role in making Buddhism the national religion of Silla, and established a profound tradition of scholarship, which is admired to this day by modern-day scholars and philosophers.

His writings can be divided into various sub-topics – Hwajaeng, Pure Land, Buddha Womb, Flower Ornament, and One Mind – all of which are connected with one another. His beliefs were not separate from his way of life. His deeds of non-hindrance and compassion expressed the essence of his beliefs all the more clearly. Thus, his life represents a source of insight and a bridge between past and present, as the problems and conflicts faced by Master Wonhyo in Silla 1300 years ago are equally apparent in modern times.

Wonhyo was born in 617 A.D., exactly 90 years after Buddhism became an officially recognised religion in the country. At that time, Silla Buddhism was employed by the government as a means for developing the country and furthering the cause of national unification.

Located in the southern corner of the Korean peninsula, Silla was traditionally a closed and socially conservative society, studiously avoiding the influence of other cultures. Buddhism entered into Silla with great difficulty, and there are even accounts of the Koguryo Buddhist missionaries Chongbang and Myolkuja being put to death. The formal recognition of Buddhism by King Pophung occurred only after the martyrdom of the monk Ichadon, a member of the Silla royal family, and even this occurred 150 years after Buddhism had been recognized by Koguryo and Paekche, the other two ancient kingdoms of the Korean peninsula.

Once accepted, however, its development was nurtured by the royal government with astounding zeal. King Pophung issued a national proclamation which prohibited the killing of animals in 529 (the 16th year of his reign). King Chinhung, who succeeded Pophung, encouraged his people to take up holy orders and become monks. The country also started construction of many grand temples such as Hwangnyongsa and Chiwonsa, and invited renowned clerics from Silla and abroad to give lectures and take part in religious ceremonies. During this time, Silla formed an elite corps known as Hwarangdo in order to train competent young men for the service of their country, and Buddhism was used to provide for the spiritual aspect of their training.

Silla Buddhism during this initial period could be criticized for placing more emphasis on national development than what might be considered true Buddhist practice, particularly as the secular motives of the state did not always correspond with those of the Buddhist faith. Furthermore, as various sects and schools of Buddhism were introduced to Korea, Silla Buddhism faced the challenge of systematizing the various doctrines which often conflicted with one another. While the basic elements of Buddhist philosophy apply universally to everyone, there are many different methods of practice, and different teachings apply to different individuals depending on their situation and spiritual level. Thus, Buddhism has many scriptures, each with a different answer to the same question. This diversity within Buddhism has naturally resulted in disputes between different sects and schools, and makes comprehension difficult for ordinary people. Wonhyo, regarding all of these problems as his own and attempting to solve them one by one, established a non-sectarian, all-inclusive form of Korean Buddhism. The spirit of Master Wonhyo has endured to this day, and as a result, Korean Buddhism is distinctively ecumenical, and is known for the harmonious coexistence of individual schools and doctrines.

2. Wonhyo's Buddhist Philosophy

(1) Hwajaeng (Harmonizing Disputations)

Attempting to dispel the sectarian approach to Buddhist teaching and avoid doctrinal arguments, Wonhyo wrote the Chong-Yo, an essential overview of 17 different sutras. 'Chong' means 'unfolding to all' and 'yo' means 'combining into one'. In other words, Chong-Yo is based on the view that Buddha's spirit is revealed in many different ways, but is ultimately one unified whole.

Wonhyo emphasized that although two sides in an argument may have reasons for their objections, both should attempt to view the situation in a rounded and holistic way. He expressed the concept of Hwajaeng in *Yolbangyong Chongyo* (Fundamental Essence of Nirvana Sutra), "If you synthesize the many elements contained within the sutras, it becomes clear that countless ideas all come back to one meaning. If one distils this universal meaning, it is possible to harmonize the opinions of a hundred sects".

Wonhyo's Hwajaeng philosophy suggests that one should neither contradict nor affirm a given doctrine or opinion, as it is possible to bring the two sides together. This is done by considering two factors - emotion (情) and reason (理). 'Emotion' here refers to the feeling of attachment to one's own opinion which insists "I am right". While acknowledging everyone's attachment to his or her own beliefs and accepting these feelings, one can make apparent the limitations of a given viewpoint with respect to the whole, and thus allow each person to recognize the wisdom of not holding on to a narrow viewpoint. This latter process is the way of reason (理). Hwajaeng, in short, means to affirm both sides and contradict them at the same time. This is possible to achieve by embracing all that is relative and revealing the absolute that lies within.

The principle which supports the doctrine of Hwajaeng is 'One Mind'. The sea of One Mind, as Wonhyo says, is an absolute state far removed from relative discrimination. We normally understand the absolute as being the opposite of the relative, but Wonhyo's concept of the transcendental absolute goes beyond the state of opposition.

(2) Ilsim (One Mind)

Throughout Wonhyo's works, the idea of 'returning to the source of One Mind' often recurs. All sentient beings exist within the One Mind; however, because we have forgotten this, we must 'return to the source of One Mind'. The aim is to awaken reverence and compassion within us, since all beings are endowed with One Mind, the 'repository of Buddha-nature'.

In order to be capable of returning to the source of One Mind, we must first understand the mind. According to the *Awakening of Faith*, our mind consists of two gates, i.e. the True-Suchness Gate (眞如門) and the Arising-Ceasing Gate (生滅門). The True-Suchness Gate is the centrepoint of the Essence that is removed from all discriminations; the Arising-Ceasing Gate is the world of phenomena projected by discriminations. Wonhyo explains that "the True-Suchness Gate and Arising-Ceasing Gate encompass the entire dharma. Therefore, the two gates are not separate. Buddha Nature is hidden within the Arising-Ceasing Gate". Viewed from the perspective of One Mind, all discriminations are removed and all things are equal.

The essence of Buddha Nature is the One Mind. The nature of One Mind is set apart from all discriminations. Being apart from all discriminations, the One Mind does not correspond to anything. Not having correspondence to anything, One Mind does not correspond to nothing.

- Fundamental Essence of the Nirvana Sutra

The fountainhead of One Mind, which is distinct from existence and nonexistence, is independently pure. The sea of the Three Voids, which combines the absolute and worldly, is calm and clear. Calm and clear, it combines duality and yet is not unitary. Independently pure, it is far from extremes and yet is not found at the mid-point. It is not found at the mid-point and yet it is far from the extremes. Hence, a phenomenon that does not exist does not merely abide in nonexistence; and that which does not non-exist does not merely abide in existence.

- Exposition of the Vajrasamadhi Sutra

The passage above states that the One Mind combines the absolute and the worldly. Wonhyo's purpose of re-iterating the concept of One Mind is to reveal the true mind, which is above all suffering, and abides in a liberated state without attachment. As the text reads, "that which does not non-exist does not merely abide in existence". If the One Mind is considered to be a fixed reality, it cannot be reached. In Wonhyo's words, "It transcends both speech and thought. Therefore, not knowing how to name it, I am obliged to call it One Mind". (*Fundamental Essence of the Nirvana Sutra*)

As the absolute and the worldly are brought together by means of the One Mind, the cycle of birth and death and Nirvana become non-dual. Furthermore, the world of birth and death and the Pure Land of Nirvana reside together in the

One Mind. Likewise, the world of sentient beings and the world of Buddha both proceed from the One Mind. Once we realize this, our One Mind will have recovered its essence. While we do not realize this, we cannot help but live as ignorant sentient beings. We are with One Mind, and yet we are without One Mind. This is the reality of worldly life and sentient existence.

(3) Muae (Non Hindrance)

Muae (Non Hindrance) is the consummation of Wonhyo's thought in action. Muae stands for freedom, unconfined by dualistic opposites and fixed conventions. It is different from pursuing individual desires, as it is rooted in One Mind, which evokes balance and compassion within us. In other words, Muae means that one is no longer bound by the duality of 'self' and 'others', and can live a compassionate life.

From the perspective of Buddhism, freedom without compassion is not real freedom, but self-indulgence. Compassion without freedom, on the other hand, is passive and not true compassion. If we attain one, we naturally come to attain the other. Freedom and compassion are inseparable in Muae. It is not based on atomistic and possessive individualism, but is rooted in the unification of 'you' and 'I'. Muae aims at benefitting both oneself and others, and this touches the heart of Buddhism, 'the great compassion of unity'.

(4) The Pure Land

Wonhyo was a proponent of Pure Land Buddhism and incorporated it fully into his teachings. Pure Land theory was closely connected with the theory of Hwajaeng and One Mind. With respect to personal enlightenment, the Hwajaeng and One Mind philosophy suggest that anyone can attain enlightenment through means appropriate to their situation and spiritual level.

This view, which stresses the equality of all beings in regard to attaining Buddhahood, was at odds with the spirit of early Silla Buddhism, which looked to justify the social hierarchy by placing emphasis on the concept of *karma*[8]. According to Wonhyo, the door leading to absolute Truth is open to all. This challenged the typical view of the lay follower as a passive subject, rather than an active participant in the spiritual path for enlightenment.

The Pure Land where Amitabha Buddha resides is an ideal celestial realm and 'pure abode'. Anyone who purifies his or her mind by chanting the name of Amitabha Buddha with reverence is able to enter the Pure Land after death, regardless of age, gender or social class. Because Pure Land Buddhism was easy to understand and practice, it spoke to those who were not well-versed in the more complex aspects of Buddhist philosophy and practice. This is why Wonhyo chose this simple and approachable belief to propagate Buddhism amongst ordinary people.

3. Wonhyo's Lessons for Today

Wonhyo's theory of Hwajaeng was the product of his own reflections on history. Using it as a basis, he harmonized and resolved the opposing views he saw in the Buddhist world. Practitioners were being diverted from attaining Buddha's true teaching as a result of the conflict between Voidness Buddhism and Consciousness-Only Buddhism. Thanks to the theory of Hwajaeng, Buddhist philosophy in Silla did not waste further time on fruitless discussions, but was able to develop further.

---

[8] *Karma* (Sanskrit). Any kind of physical, vocal, or mental action that is imprinted in the mind and subsequently gives rise to certain consequences in the future. Karmic action can be positive or negative, intentional and unintentional.

Furthermore, through his theory of One Mind, which served as the basis for the Hwajaeng philosophy, Wonhyo emphasized that the world of Nirvana does not exist separately from this world, and that consequently, the world where we live can also be realm of the absolute. Wonhyo insisted that anyone who realizes the truth of the One Mind can be enlightened in this world.

Wonhyo also thought that the ultimate purpose of Buddhism was to rescue sentient beings from suffering. However great a theory may be, if it is not applied in our daily lives, it is lifeless and useless. His own life is a perfect example of the propagation of Buddhism based on philosophical truth and the coming together of theory and practice. In this sense, the life and works of Wonhyo, a pillar of Korean Buddhism, remain a source of guidance and inspiration for us today.

IX. Laying Down His Pen

Wonhyo's thought is based on a universal contemplation of life. It cannot be expressed by a religious text or captured in a metaphysical system. It does not deal in simple opposites such as real and ideal, material and spiritual, individual and whole, existent and nonexistent, or good and evil. In spite of its logical and systematic framework, it remains a broad and profound reflection on the essence of being, with a non-hindered life as its aim.

Specialization, one of the driving forces behind civilization today, has come at the expense of relationships between individuals in human society. The human being has become alienated, and our cultural intake unbalanced. As the world faces conflicts between different civilisations, a new and more broad-minded outlook is vital. The role of art and philosophy today is to reflect reality and overcome the fragmentation that has occurred within society.

Until the last century, philosophers were concerned with questions of 'existence', asking what the nature of human life really is, and to what extent man's behavior towards his fellow man can be an influence for good or evil. In the 21st century, we are faced with a new challenge in the form of a global environmental crisis. Moreover, advances in cloning techniques and genetic engineering, and innovations such as the replacement of human organs with artificial devices, are forcing us to re-assess societal norms. Pollution and global warming are problems that require a united response. Changing ecosystems threaten the very survival of the human race. The only way forward is to approach the crisis as one world and deal with it together.

Alternatively put, we must have the wisdom to see the forest rather than the individual trees. In this respect, Wonhyo's life and philosophy hold a special significance for us. His philosophy is based on a realization of the value of individual life. Practice, not theory, is the key to his One Mind and Hwajaeng philosophy.

Extracts from Wonhyo's Writings

Sentient beings and Buddha Nature are not the same, and yet they are not different.

〈금강삼매경론〉

One who realizes that he is in delusion is not greatly deluded, and one who realizes that he is in darkness is not in total darkness.

〈보살계본지범요기〉

The wrong vanishes on its own while the right reveals itself, just as the real gold will shine on its own, while the imitation will not.

〈대승기신론소〉

I wish to use words to show the Dharma that is beyond words, just like using a finger to point at the moon, which is separate from the finger.

〈십문화쟁론〉

When sewing clothes, a short needle is needed, and a long spear is useless.
To avoid the rain, a small umbrella is needed, and a cover that spans the entire sky is useless.
Therefore, small things should not be regarded as trivial.
Depending on their true nature, both small and large things are precious.

〈미륵상생경종요〉

The sun has heat as its basic nature, and the moon has cold as its basic nature.
If there is only the sun, and no moon, the growing shoots will dry up and will not live long enough to bear fruit. But if there is only the moon and no sun, the shoots cannot grow and so will rot.

〈범망경보살계본사기〉

The virtuous merit of repentance is praised as being pure and cool.

Because it cleanses impurity, which is the cause of wrong, it is pure.

By forgoing the heat of carnal desire, which proceeds from endless life and death, it is cool.

<금강삼매경론>

To practice internally means to practice watching the mind in quiet reflection.

To practice externally means to come out of watching the mind, and to transform others through teaching them.

Whether one enters or comes out [of the practice], because it [the practice] does not digress from the Middle Way, it is spoken of as not being either of the two.

<금강삼매경론>

The boundless wisdom of Mahayana (Great Vehicle) is, simply, the Sacred Wisdom of Equality of All Things. Because it dwells in 'no I', there is nothing that is not 'I'. Because there is nothing that is not 'I', there is nothing that it does not embrace equally. Empowered with the wisdom that all beings have the same original nature, it carries countless sentient beings towards the great enlightenment. For this reason, it is called the boundless wisdom of Mahayana (Great Vehicle).

<무량수경종요>

Some people put forward their limited views based on a little experience, and are pleased if others agree with their views. But if others disagree, they criticize them. They are like people who observe the sky through a hollow reed. They claim that looking at the sky through a hollow reed is good, and that others who do not view the sky in this way cannot see the sky. This is the ignorance of believing oneself to be wise, though lacking insight, and criticizing those with greater wisdom.

<보살계본지범요기>

While wise and holy men perform many virtuous acts, they adopt these seven practices for the training of their character. Faith, the foundation of many virtues; Giving, to double the benefit; Observance of Precepts, to avoid disasters easily; Listening, to gather all that is of value; Repentance, to revere and increase what is good; Shame, to keep wickedness far from them; and Wisdom, to control and augment the six riches.

<본업경소>

To have faith means to conclusively affirm the state of things. In other words, to truly believe in the existence of the Dharma, to believe that it can be attained through the practice, and that when one attains it through practice, it brings boundless virtue and merit.

<대승기신론소>

A hindrance is a block in one's path, but it also means 'to obscure'. Karmic hindrance blocks the path of sentient beings so that they cannot escape the cycle of birth and death. It also envelops sentient beings, and so hides nirvana. For these two reasons, it is called 'hindrance'.

<이장의>

The mindset which is neither ashamed nor afraid of sin is the source of all non-goodness.

<유가사지론>

If one commits one of these four errors, one cannot be part of a community,

And one must leave it.

The first is to praise oneself and disparage others.

The second is to be mean with one's wealth or knowledge, and hold it only for oneself without sharing it with others.

The third is to hold anger within and not to accept others apologies and repentance.

The fourth is to criticize the true Dharma and cause confusion.

<유가사지론>

If you are lacking in even one of the virtues, you cannot attain complete enlightenment.

In order to return to the fundamental cause, you must be equipped with every form of discipline.

<대승기신론소>

A great person's character is lofty and broad. Its spirit is simple and without boundaries. [Such a spirit] treats disaster and good fortune alike, and makes no distinction between "I" and "others". This spirit is always blissful, and dwells in righteousness. Consequently, one does not praise oneself and criticize others, nor put oneself forward and suppress others.

<보살계본지범요기>

The Awakening of Faith and Practice

The Buddhas reside in majesty at the Palace of Extinction, Nirvana, because they have renounced attachments and practiced austerities over a long period. Meanwhile, innumerable sentient beings are reincarnated within the walls of the blazing house, Samsara, and refuse to renounce their greed for countless eons.

The path to Heaven is unobstructed, and yet few reach it, because many regard the Three Poisons[9] and Defilements as treasures. Many go out of their way to enter the evil realms, although these realms have no allurements, because they regard the Four Elements[10] and the Five Desires[11] as the riches of the mind.

Who would not wish to dwell in the mountains and cultivate the mind? And yet you cannot do so, because you are enslaved to desire. Even if you cannot return to the forests and mountains to practice, you should do the best you can, and never abandon the practice of good deeds. If you willingly abandon your desires like this, you will be trusted and respected as the sages are; and if you willingly practice what is difficult, you will be revered as Lord Buddha is revered. To grasp and covet material things is the way of the Maras; to give with compassion is the way of the Dharma King.

High mountains and rough peaks are where wise men dwell. Green pines and deep mountain valleys are home to those who practice. When hungry, they pick

---

[9] Greed, anger and arrogance (ignorance).
[10] The elements of earth, water, fire and air that constitute our physical bodies. To attach oneself to the Four Elements therefore means to be attached to the body.
[11] The desire for food, fame, wealth, lust and sleep.

fruit from trees to calm an empty stomach. When thirsty, they quench their thirst with water from the running stream. Though we feed this body with fine delicacies and nurture it with care, in the end it is certain to fail us. And though we may cover it with fine clothes, the time will come when our lives must cease.

A rocky cave that resonates with echoing sounds, make this your hall of recitation. The wild geese that cry in solitude, make these the joyful companions of your mind. Though your knees are cold and numb from continual bowing, have no thought for a fire. Though your empty stomach feels severed from your body, have no thought to look for food. Before you know it, you will be a hundred years old, so why do you neglect to learn? Could life ever be long enough for us to idle it away and neglect our studies?

When your heart is emptied of longing, you are a sramana[12]. Giving no thought to worldly things is renunciation of the world. For a practitioner to be caught in the net of desire is like a dog wearing the hide of an elephant. A practitioner who yearns after lustful desires is like a hedgehog that enters a mouse-hole. For those who live at home in the village, even though they have great wisdom and ability, all the Buddhas are sad and concerned for them. For those who stay in the depths of mountains, even though they do not practice the Dharma, many saints feel great joy because of them.

Although talented and able, one who does not follow the precepts is like one who, having been led to a place of treasure, stands still and goes no further. Though diligent in practice, one who lacks wisdom is like one who travels west when he should go east. The wise man steams rice to eat, while the ignorant man steams

---

[12] Sramana is one who renounces the world and leads a life of austerity with the aim of spiritual development and liberation.

sand. Everyone knows how to cure a hungry stomach by eating food, yet no one knows how to cure the ignorance of the mind through learning the Dharma. Wisdom and Practice are like the two wheels of a cart. To benefit oneself and benefit others – these are like the two wings of a bird.

You may offer prayers having received your rice, but if you do not know the meaning of your words, is this not something to be ashamed of before the giver? Even though you chant the prayer of offering at a meal, if you do not understand its importance, is this not also something to be ashamed of before the Sages? Maggots are hated because they make no distinction between clean and unclean. Similarly, Bodhisattvas have no delight in monks who cannot distinguish between actions that are pure and actions that go against the precepts. If one wishes to leave behind the chaos of the world, to ascend to the upper air and be born in the heavens, the precepts are a good ladder. Aspiring to be a field of merit for others, while going against the precepts, is like a bird that tries to fly with broken wings carrying a turtle on its back.[13] If you are still in the shadow of your own sins, you cannot free others from their sins. For this reason, if you do not carry out the precepts, how can you receive respect and offerings from another? There is no benefit in nourishing an empty body that does not cultivate the mind, and a transient and futile life is difficult to preserve, however much one tends to it.

To aspire to the virtues of the great masters, you must willingly endure suffering

---

[13] Monks do not work to earn their living but depend on the offerings of the lay-followers. Master Wonhyo is reproaching those who do not follow the precepts, but accept offerings nevertheless. Making an offering to a practitioner who studies well becomes merit; hence they are a 'field of merit', allowing others to practice good deeds. Donations to practitioners who study badly do not become merit, and this is a stern rebuke to such practitioners who are ignorant of this fact.

at great length. To aspire to the Lion's Seat[14], you must forever turn your back on the Five Desires. When a practitioner's mind is pure, the Heavens greatly admire it, and if one who walks the path turns his mind to lustful thoughts, the good spirits will desert and leave him. The Four Elements will unexpectedly scatter, and you will not be able to preserve them for long. Soon it will be evening, and we should have been practicing since dawn! Indulging in the pleasures of this life will bring suffering in a later life, so why should we yearn after them? Refraining from them even one time will bring a lasting future joy, so why do we not cultivate the mind? The desires of a spiritual seeker are the shame of a practitioner, and the wealth of one who has renounced the world is a source of mockery for the worldly folk he has left behind.

Though cautioned unceasingly with endless words, we do not desist in our desires. Though we constantly make resolutions, we do not sever our attachments. Although there is nothing to lose, no one is willing to let go of worldly concerns; and although there is no end to delusion, none can bring themselves to cut their ties. Today has not yet ended, but is already tainted with many sins. So the days of sin are many, and there is no end to the tomorrows when we must face the consequences of our actions. And yet the days of good deeds are few. Though the year has yet to end, it is full of sufferings because we have sinned without ceasing. Though there are many years to come, we do not cultivate wisdom and prepare ourselves for the future.

Hour after hour passes, and the day is swiftly gone. Days pass, and the last day of the month is already here. The months pass, and a new year is upon us. The years pass, and before long we stand at the threshold of death. Just as a broken cart cannot move, in old age one cannot practice. And yet we sit in passive

---

[14] The seat from which Buddha or Enlightened Masters give Dharma Lectures.

idleness, allowing our thoughts to wander.

The lives we have spent in practice are few, and yet today we do not practice, letting the time pass by in vain. How futile this body is, and yet you do not use this life to study. This life will soon come to an end, and if the end comes without practice, what body will you receive next? Is it not serious? Are you not afraid?

Author Jeong, Byeong-Jo

Professor Jeong graduated from the Department of Indian Philosophy at Dongguk University and received his doctoral degree in 1986, with a dissertation entitled "Study on Mañjuśrī Bodhisattva". He has been a professor at the Department of Ethical Culture at Dongguk University since 1980. He is a former vice president of the university, and spent two years as a visiting professor at Nehru University in India (1984-1986). As the president and chairman of the Korea Institute of Buddhist Studies (KIBS), he endeavors to promote academic interchange between Korea, the US and Europe in the field of Buddhist studies. His writings include *A History of Indian Philosophical Thought*, *Theory on the History of Buddhist Culture*, *Practical Buddhism*, *A History of Korean Buddhist Thought*, and his papers include 'Study on Avalokitesvara with Eleven Faces', 'Study on Woncheuk's Praise to Heart Sutra', and 'Study on the Layperson's Buddhist Movement in Modern Korea'.